W9-AOS-011

January/Enero

By/Por Robyn Brode

Reading Consultant/Consultora de lectura: Linda Cornwell,
Literacy Connections Consulting/consultora de lectoescritura

WEEKLY READER®
PUBLISHING

Please visit our web site at **www.garethstevens.com**.
For a free catalog describing our list of high-quality books, call 1-800-542-2595 (USA)
or 1-800-387-3178 (Canada). Our fax: 1-877-542-2596

Library of Congress Cataloging-in-Publication Data
Brode, Robyn.
  [January. Spanish & English]
  January / by Robyn Brode ; reading consultant, Linda Cornwell = Enero / por Robyn Brode ;
consultora de lectura, Linda Cornwell.
      p. cm. — (Months of the year = Meses del año)
  Includes bibliographical references and index.
  ISBN-10: 1-4339-1929-X   ISBN-13: 978-1-4339-1929-9 (lib. bdg.)
  ISBN-10: 1-4339-2106-5   ISBN-13: 978-1-4339-2106-3 (softcover)
    1. January—Juvenile literature.   2. Holidays—United States—Juvenile literature.
  3. Winter—United States—Juvenile literature.   I. Cornwell, Linda.   II. Title.   III. Title: Enero.
  GT4803.B766   2010b
  394.261—dc22   2009012682

This edition first published in 2010 by
Weekly Reader® Books
An Imprint of Gareth Stevens Publishing
1 Reader's Digest Road
Pleasantville, NY 10570-7000 USA

Copyright © 2010 by Gareth Stevens, Inc.

Executive Managing Editor: Lisa M. Herrington
Senior Editors: Barbara Bakowski, Jennifer Magid-Schiller
Designer: Jennifer Ryder-Talbot
Translators: Tatiana Acosta and Guillermo Gutiérrez

Photo Credits: Cover, back cover, title, pp. 9, 11 (left), 19 © Ariel Skelley/Weekly Reader; pp. 7, 21
© Masterfile; p. 11 (right) © Getty Images; p. 13 © letty17/Shutterstock; p. 15 © Christophe Testi/
Shutterstock; p. 17 © Hulton Archive/Getty Images

Printed in the United States of America

1 2 3 4 5 6 7 8 9 10 11 10 09

Table of Contents/Contenido

Boldface words appear in the glossary.

Las palabras en **negrita** aparecen en el glosario.

Happy New Year!

January is the first month of the year.

January has 31 days.

— — — — — — — — —

¡Feliz Año Nuevo!

Enero es el primer mes del año.

Enero tiene 31 días.

Months of the Year/Meses del año

Month/Mes	Number of Days/ Días en el mes
1 January/Enero	31
2 February/Febrero	28 or 29*/28 ó 29*
3 March/Marzo	31
4 April/Abril	30
5 May/Mayo	31
6 June/Junio	30
7 July/Julio	31
8 August/Agosto	31
9 September/Septiembre	30
10 October/Octubre	31
11 November/Noviembre	30
12 December/Diciembre	31

*February has an extra day every fourth year./Febrero tiene un día extra cada cuatro años. **5**

January 1 is called **New Year's Day**.
People celebrate the start of the new year.

— — — — — — — — — —

El 1 de enero es el **Día de Año Nuevo**.
Ese día celebramos el comienzo de un
nuevo año.

Winter **vacation** ends in January. It is time to go back to school.

— — — — — — — —

Las **vacaciones** de invierno terminan en enero. Es el momento de volver a la escuela.

9

Winter Weather

January is a **winter** month. Some places are cold and snowy in winter. Others are warm.

– – – – – – – – –

Tiempo de invierno

Enero es uno de los meses de **invierno**. En invierno, en algunos lugares hace frío y nieva. En otros hace buen tiempo.

What is the weather like in January where you live?

– – – – – – –

¿Qué tiempo hace en enero en el lugar donde vives?

10

In some places, people go ice-skating during the winter. They wear special shoes called **ice skates**.

- - - - - - - - - -

En algunos lugares, la gente sale en invierno a patinar sobre hielo. Para patinar, se usan unos zapatos especiales llamados **patines de hielo**.

ice skates/
patines de hielo

13

Special Days

In some years, Chinese New Year begins in January. People celebrate for 15 days. They watch **parades** with colorful dragons.

— — — — — — — — — —

Días especiales

Algunos años, el Año Nuevo Chino empieza en enero. Las celebraciones duran 15 días. La gente sale a ver **desfiles** de dragones de colores.

In January, we celebrate the birthday of Martin Luther King Jr. He was a leader who wanted all people to be treated the same.

– – – – – – – – –

En enero, celebramos el cumpleaños de Martin Luther King Jr. Este líder quería que todas las personas fueran tratadas de la misma manera.

Martin Luther King Jr.

17

Students learn about King in school. They think about his message of hope for the future.

– – – – – – – – – –

En la escuela, se estudia a Martin Luther King Jr. Los estudiantes aprenden su mensaje de esperanza para el futuro.

When January ends, it is time for February to begin.

— — — — — — — — —

Cuando enero termina, empieza febrero.

Glossary/Glosario

ice skates: special shoes with a blade on the bottom that people wear to glide on ice

New Year's Day: a holiday that falls on the first day of a calendar year

parades: marches in honor of a person or an event. Parades often include musical bands, floats, and people in costumes.

vacation: time away from school or work

winter: the season between fall and spring. It is usually the coldest time of the year.

— — — — — — — — —

desfiles: marchas que se celebran para conmemorar a una persona o un suceso. En los desfiles suele haber bandas musicales, carrozas y gente disfrazada.

Día de Año Nuevo: fiesta que se celebra el primer día del año

invierno: la estación del año entre el otoño y la primavera. Suele ser la época más fría del año.

patines de hielo: zapatos especiales con una cuchilla en la suela, que la gente se pone para deslizarse sobre el hielo

vacaciones: periodo de descanso de las actividades de la escuela o del trabajo

For More Information/Más información

Books/Libros

Martin Luther King Jr. Day/Día de Martin Luther King Jr.
Our Country's Holidays/Las fiestas de nuestra nación
(series). Sheri Dean (Gareth Stevens Publishing, 2006)

Winter/Invierno. Seasons of the Year/Las estaciones del año
(series). JoAnn Early Macken (Gareth Stevens Publishing, 2006)

Web Sites/Páginas web

Chinese New Year/Año Nuevo Chino
www.history.com/minisites/chinesenewyear
Watch a video about Chinese New Year traditions./Vean un video
de las tradiciones del Año Nuevo Chino.

Martin Luther King Jr.
seattletimes.nwsource.com/special/mlk
Learn all about Martin Luther King Jr./Conozcan mejor a
Martin Luther King Jr.

Index/Índice

About the Author

Robyn Brode has been a teacher, a writer, and an editor in the book publishing field for many years. She earned a bachelor's degree in English literature from the University of California, Berkeley.

Información sobre la autora

Robyn Brode ha sido maestra, escritora y editora de libros durante muchos años. Obtuvo su licenciatura en literatura inglesa en la Universidad de California, Berkeley.